One day Kevin and Lotty are sniffing in the long grass.

Sniff, sniff goes Kevin.

Sniff, sniff goes Lotty.

They can smell a fox.

Kevin runs after the smell.

Lotty runs after the smell.

Sniff, sniff. Sniff, sniff.

The two dogs run fast.

All of a sudden, they are at the top of a pit.

They can see Chuff in the pit with a fox cub.

Chuff and the fox cub are stuck at the bottom of the pit.

They cannot get out.

Kevin and Lotty must help them.

The dogs see a log on the grass.

They push it to the pit.

They push and they push.

They huff and they puff.

Then one end of the log falls into the pit.

Chuff picks up the fox cub.

He gets on to the log with it.

Chuff and the fox cub go up the log.

They get to the top of the pit.

Chuff puts the fox cub on the grass.

The fox cub runs off to look for his mum.

Kevin and Lotty go back to the shed with Chuff.

They are all happy.